NUMBER QUEST

An adventure in mathematics

NUMBER QUEST

**by
Dr Michael Thomson
with mathematics problems from
Ann Power**

Illustrated by Bryony Jacklin

To Jamie, with love.

Number Quest
LD 955
ISBN 1-85503-115-9
© Text Michael Thomson
© Illustrations Bryony Jacklin
All rights reserved
First published 1991
Reprinted 1993, 1994
LDA, Duke Street, Wisbech, Cambs. PE13 2AE, England.

READ THIS FIRST!

You are the star in this adventure story. When you read Number Quest you will be on a quest to use the power of mathematics to defy RA, the terror of the Pyramid. You will fight off Multiplying Hound, meet the Mummy in the Tomb and save the Dancing Skeletons. You will ward off the Divider Spiders, beat off the Bracket Bats and free the Graph children.

As you go through the adventure you will be asked to do number tasks. You may need to get your answers checked by your teacher or your teacher may give you some answers so you can check yourself. As you go along you will be given clues and you will find things that will help you.

There is a very important piece of paper at the back of the book. It is your Equipment List. You can get this photocopied if you need to. In your adventure story you will find things to help you. You must write down the equipment number too so you can find it when you need it. If you do not have the right equipment you will have to go back to find it.

To begin the adventure story start at the story number with **1** at the top. You will be told what to do next at the end of the story number. This could be to go on to another story number. You might be asked to choose where you want to go next or sometimes you will have to do a number task before you go on.

Number Quest is the second of two books. The first one is called The Book of Numbers. Now read on.

GOOD LUCK!

1

Number Quest is the follow on from The Book of Numbers. It will help if you have read The Book of Numbers first. If you have, you will know that someone is trying to take the Numbers of the World away. You have travelled across a huge desert to find out who. You have had many adventures with Counting Camel and other friends. At last you have arrived at the Pyramid. The evil Dragon had gone into the Pyramid. It told you that its master was inside. You have broken the Code to let you enter the Pyramid. You are now standing by the door. Will you enter the Pyramid? If you have not read the Book of Numbers go to **60**. If you have, go to **24**.

2

This is not good news! The Mummy grabs you. A hug from this Mummy will mash you into mince meat. You run out of the room and go to look for the High Graph Priest. Go to **83** first to get the High Graph Priest. Then go back to **127**.

3

The Skeletons carry on with their dancing. The stone door that you came in has shut again. You cannot get out that way. In the far corner of the room you see a trap door. In the other corner you see an iron gate. You can go to the trap door - **19** - or go to the iron gate - **27**.

4

You take the stairs to the left. You go up a winding stone staircase. It seems to go round and round for a long time. At last you see daylight at the top of the stairs. The smell gets stronger. Go to **87**.

5

You charge at the door. It does not open. You hurt your shoulder. Go back to **16** and try again.

6

The frame tips over. The Globe is almost out. You need to do a few more sums to get the Globe out. Do these:

$23 + 78 =$ $234 + 72 =$ $343 + 728 =$

Keep trying until you get them right. Then go to **68**.

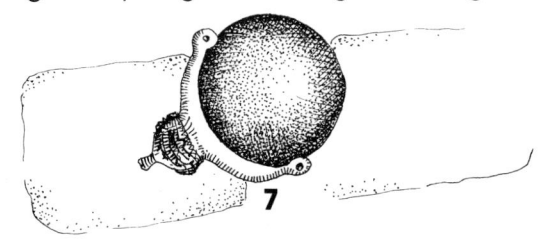

7

The Time Clock will help you with the Dragon. You look at the clock. It says:

Most timetables and some clocks are 24 hour. The 24 hour clock times are written using four numbers. For example, 06.20 is 6.20 am and 14.45 is the same as 2.45 pm. The point separates the hours from the minutes. The 12 hour clock uses only 12 hours and you have to say if it is before noon (am) or after noon (pm)

Now go to **10**.

8

The Witch cackles. 'Ha! You cannot do them, eh! You will have to die.'

She points the Mace at you. Quickly average these numbers: 12, 24, 30, 36, 48. Write down the answer below.

_____

Now go to **9**.

9

If you were correct, go on to **71**. If you made a mistake, the red light from the Mace burns into you. What a painful death!

10

The Dragon stops still. It looks at you. 'Well, human', it purrs. 'You have done well so far. Now I will ask you some riddles about Time.'

Dragons often ask riddles. They can be fun, but Dragons tend to eat people who do not get them correct. You can use the Time Clock to help you answer these riddles:

Write these as 24 hour clock times:

1	6.00 am	_____	4	2.54 pm	_____
2	9.15 am	_____	5	10.38 pm	_____
3	3.07 am	_____	6	Noon	_____

Now change these to 12 hour clock times:

7 03.21 _____   10 00.30 _____

8 16.38 _____   11 06.15 _____

9 15.41 _____   12 11.59 _____

Check your answers. If you were correct, go to **141**.
If you made mistakes, go to **15**.

11

You reach out to press the switch. It is a little stiff. You press harder. All at once water comes out of the Dragon's mouth. You put some in your water canteen. It tastes good - fresh and clear. Then the eyes of the Dragon light up. The jewels glow red. The light from the Dragon's eyes shines deep into the bowl. Is there something there? Choose again at **143** or, if you already have the Distance Chart (check your Equipment List), you can try to find out what is in the water - **34**.

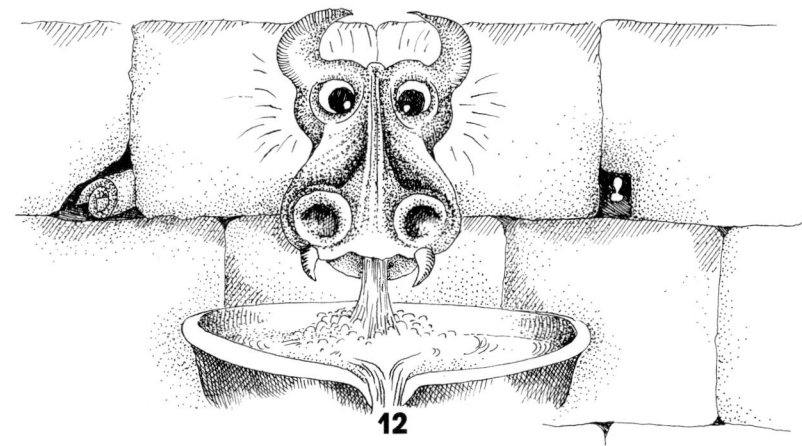

12

You leave the Mummy's Tomb. It wasn't such a bad old Mum really. You take a sharp turn down a passage you did not see before. Go to **13**.

13

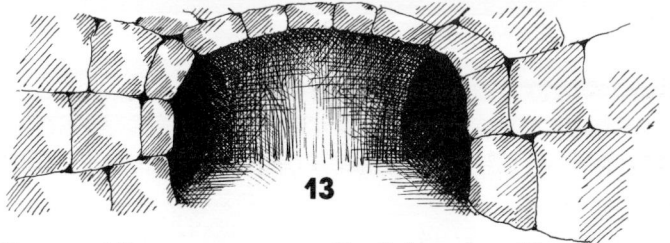

At the end the passage splits. It forms a 'T' with one way to the right and the other to the left. If you want to go to the right, go to **69**. If you want to go left, go to **37**.

14

You go down one of the passages. You lose your bearings. If you cannot find your way, you will get lost in the tunnels and die of hunger. (If the Mummy does not catch up with you first!) Go back to **138** and find your bearings again.

15

'Ha! You cannot do clocks!', says the Dragon. You had better correct the riddles at **10** before it is too late.
The Dragon is hungry.

16

You can:

- try and break the door down - **5**
- ask Number Cruncher to crunch it - **103**
- go and look for a Coin - **80**

17

You walk down the passage. After a while it ends in solid rock. This was not the way of 1927! Go back to **100** and choose again.

18

This is bad. The Multiplying Hound crunches you up. He will multiply your bones all over his den. Go back to **112** and do the sums correctly or your adventure ends here.

19

You open the trap door. There is a ladder that goes down into a dark hole. You go down to take a look. You find some old bones. There are also some numbers on the floor. They do not seem to mean anything. The Skeletons have thrown them away. You climb up the ladder and take a look at the iron gate – **27**.

20

If you wrote 'seven' or '7' go to **53**. If you wrote '77' or 'seventy-seven' go to **30**. If you wrote any other number go to **134**.

21

The High Graph Priest holds out his hands. He uses the Magic of the Seventh Son. 'By the sacred number 77 I tell you to stop! RA has made you do this. I cast the spell from you.'

A blue glow comes out of the Priest's fingers. The Mummy shakes its head. It seems to understand. The Mummy has been shut up in this small room too long. It agrees to let the children go if you will help it move into a bigger room.

You have a look at the rooms around the Mummy's Tomb. You will have to work out how big the rooms are. You need to find out which is the biggest room. Check your Equipment List. Do you have the Spell of Areas? If you do, go to **51**. If you do not, go to **102**.

22

The Skeletons are not happy. They will not let you leave until you buy something. You will have to stay here and watch the Dance of Numbers for the rest of your life unless you buy something. Go to **113**.

23

You will have to have a calendar for this riddle. It must be this year's calendar. You may have to get one from school or home. Make a note of this number. Then go and find this year's calendar. When you have done that you can come back here or go to **26**.

Do you have this year's calendar now? If you do, go to **26**.

24

The stink of stale air greets you as you go inside. You see that the walls are black. They have been flame-blasted by the Dragon. You are in a large room. It is the antechamber of the Pyramid. The room is lit by a strange light. You look up. You see a bright globe high on the wall. It is held in a metal frame. It is the Globe of Everlasting Light. It will keep on glowing as long as you do your number tasks. You will need it to explore the Pyramid. Go to **25**.

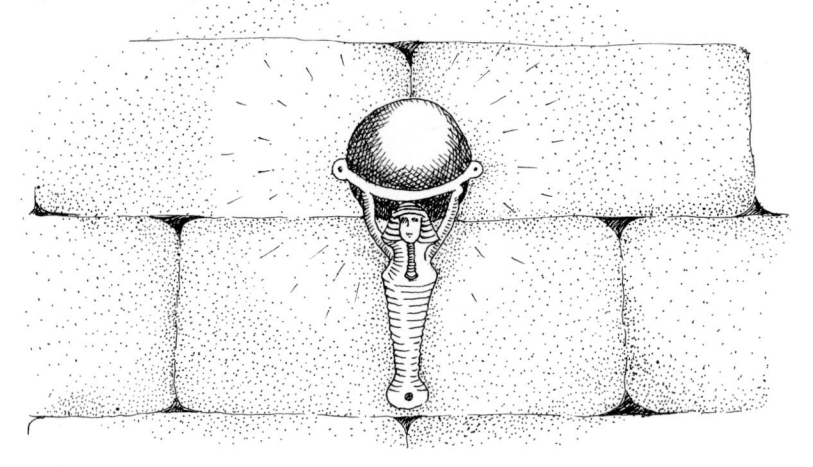

25

How will you get the Globe down from the wall? You see some numbers on the wall next to the metal frame. One set of numbers says 4 + 7. Who will help you? Choose one of your friends from The Book of Numbers.

- Adder - go to **46**
- Number Cruncher - go to **85**
- Counting Camel - go to **106**

26

You should have this year's calendar. If you do, read on and use the calendar when you need to! If you do not have a calendar, go to **23**.

The Dragon says, 'So, if you know so much about Time, answer these questions'.

1 How many months are there in a year? _____

2 Write out the names of the months that have 30 days.

3 Write out the names of the months that have 31 days.

4 Which month have you not written? _____

5 How many days are there in a year? _____

6 How many Saturdays in April? _____

7 What date is Christmas Day? _____

   What day is Christmas Day this year? _____

8 How many days are there between New Year's Day and Easter Sunday?

   _____

9 How many days are there in the last three months of the year?

   _____

10 The Dragon goes on a fortnight's burning of the town. He starts on August 10. What date does he return?

   _____

11 RA plans to destroy all the Numbers of the World a week on Monday. What date will it be and how long have you got between now and then to stop him?

   _____

Now check all your answers. If you were correct, go to **35**. If you made some mistakes, get some help and go back over the questions. When they are correct go on.

27

You go over to the iron gate. It is shut and locked. The key hole is shaped like a skull. Do you have the Skeleton Keys? Check your Equipment List. If you have the Skeleton Keys, go to **38**. If you do not have the Keys, make a note of this number and go to **115**.

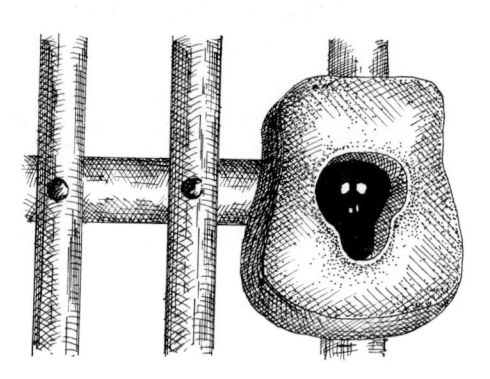

28

You should have written at least five reasons. You may need to check that they really are ways that you can use mathematics. If you were correct go to **29**.

29

'Oh!', says the Mummy. 'Well, you may need this to help you.' It goes to a small chest on the floor. It takes out a pair of curved sticks. They are Bracket Boomerangs. Write them down on your Equipment List. You thank the Mummy and turn to go – **12**.

30

You say 'The magic and elder number of yore is seventy-seven'. The Priests nod their heads. 'Yes, but what about the Graph?', they say.

They take you to the other end of the room. You see a large graph (or histogram) on the wall. You will have to use it to answer the questions the High Graph Priests ask you.

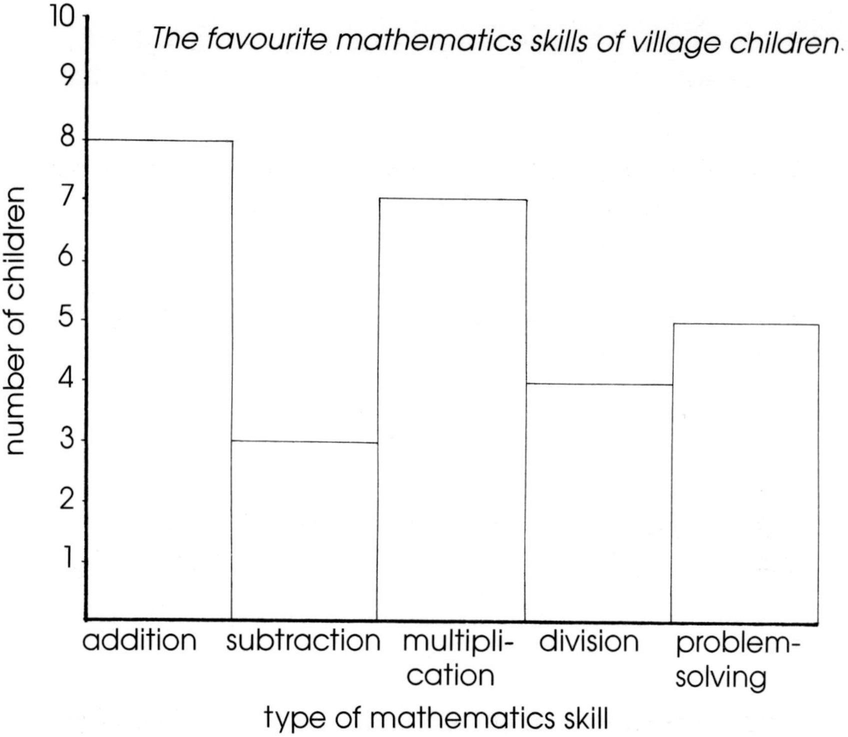
The favourite mathematics skills of village children.
number of children
10
9
8
7
6
5
4
3
2
1
addition
subtraction
multipli-
cation
division
problem-
solving
type of mathematics skill

The seven High Graph Priests say, 'The graph shows the maths skills that the children in our village like best. The children only like one thing each'. Now answer these questions:

1 How many children like multiplication? __________

2 How many children like problem-solving? __________

3 How many children altogether like addition and subtraction?

____

4 How many children prefer multiplication to subtraction?

____

5 How many children are there in the village altogether?

____

6 There are 15 boys in the village. How many girls are there?
   _____

7 Multiply the number of children that like subtraction by the number of children that like multiplication.
   What do you get? _____

Now check your answers. If you were correct, go to **43**. If you made mistakes, go to **31**.

31

The Priests are not at all happy. You will have to go back and get the answers right or you end up at **134**!

32

You slice at the other head. Now the Hound has four heads, all biting at you. This was not a good idea. Better go back to **91** or you will make a dog of a hundred heads!

33

You take the stairs to the right. You go up a winding iron staircase. It seems to go round and round for a long time. At last you see daylight at the top of the stairs. The smell gets stronger. Go to **87**.

34

You put your hand down into the water. You get ready to take it out at once. There may be something nasty down there! Then your fingers touch something. It is long and thin. It is a kind of handle! You can pull the handle to see what happens - **40** - or go back to find another way to go on - **62**.

35

The Dragon looks very upset. It starts to shake and roll about. Check your Equipment List. Do you have the Time Sword? You take it out and slash out with the blade. The Dragon roars in anger. It tries to send some numbers out in a flame. The Sword passes into the Dragon's body and the Dragon disappears. You have sent the Dragon off into Time. It will come into being another time. You have defeated the Dragon! You hear a roar of rage shake the Pyramid. RA has felt his Dragon disappear into Time. He is mad now. You will need to find his Den. You can go back down the steps - **39** - or look into a small opening in the rock face at the back of the Dragon's Lair - **45**.

36

You pick them up. Write down Dividers on your Equipment List. You wonder who the body used to be. Clutching your nose you feel it is time to move on. The smell is too much! Go to **41**.

37

You take the left hand passage. After a while you come to a doorway. A huge oak door has been smashed as if by some great force. It lies crushed and splintered on the floor. You go into the room. It is the Throne Room.

All around the room are wooden chests. Some have been smashed open. Gold, silver and jewels lie across the floor. The Throne Room is where the Treasure was kept. It was here that RA was buried. All his riches were put in the Pyramid with him.

Just as you bend over to pick up a jewel you hear a voice say, 'Not so fast, Tomb robber!'.

Your heart beats madly. The voice came from the Throne. You turn and you feel sure that RA will be sitting there. The Throne seems empty. Then, in the dim light, you make out the form of a small figure. It is an old woman. She is tiny, but looks at you with keen black eyes. 'No', she says, 'I am not RA, but I hold his Mace'.

The old woman holds up a long rod with some numbers and other signs on it. It is the Mean Old Average Witch. RA left the Mean Old Average Witch to guard his gold.

If you want some Coins you will have to find out the average (sometimes called the 'mean') of the money and riches in the Tomb. If you get this right you will also destroy the Witch.

The Witch points the Mace at you. A red light flashes out at you. What two things do you need to help you? Check your Equipment List and write down two things that might help you. Then go to **52**.

38

You take out the Skeleton Keys. One of them fits the gate. It is stiff, but you push it open. You find that you are in a cave. It stinks! You see that it is a cave where bats live. They are not here at the moment.

You are about to leave when you see a glint of metal. It seems to come from a pile of bat droppings in the corner. You can go and look to see what it is - **55** - or go on to **66**.

39

You go back down the steps. You go back to the Skeletons. They are still dancing. After a while you see that there is no way on from here. You go back up the steps. Go to **45**.

40

You pull the handle. The Dragon's eyes stop glowing. Nothing seems to happen. Then there is a grating noise. A door opens slowly next to you. A smell of death and decay greets you. This is the only way onwards. You will have to go in.

Inside is a small room with a door leading off. In the middle of the room is a low stone table. On the table lies a rag-tag roll of winding sheets. They are draped over the shape of a body. It is a Mummy. A person is buried here wrapped in cloth. It seems that the Mummy has not kept very well. The body is decaying!

In one of the Mummy's hands you see a glint of metal. As you walk over to the Mummy something falls to the ground. You see two metal rods with points at the end. The rods are joined by a hinge. It is a Pair of Dividers. You can pick them up - **36** - or go on - **41**.

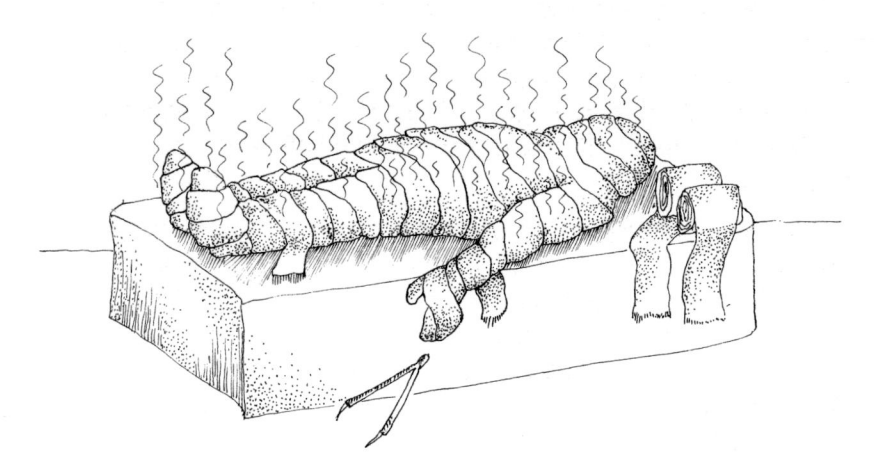

41

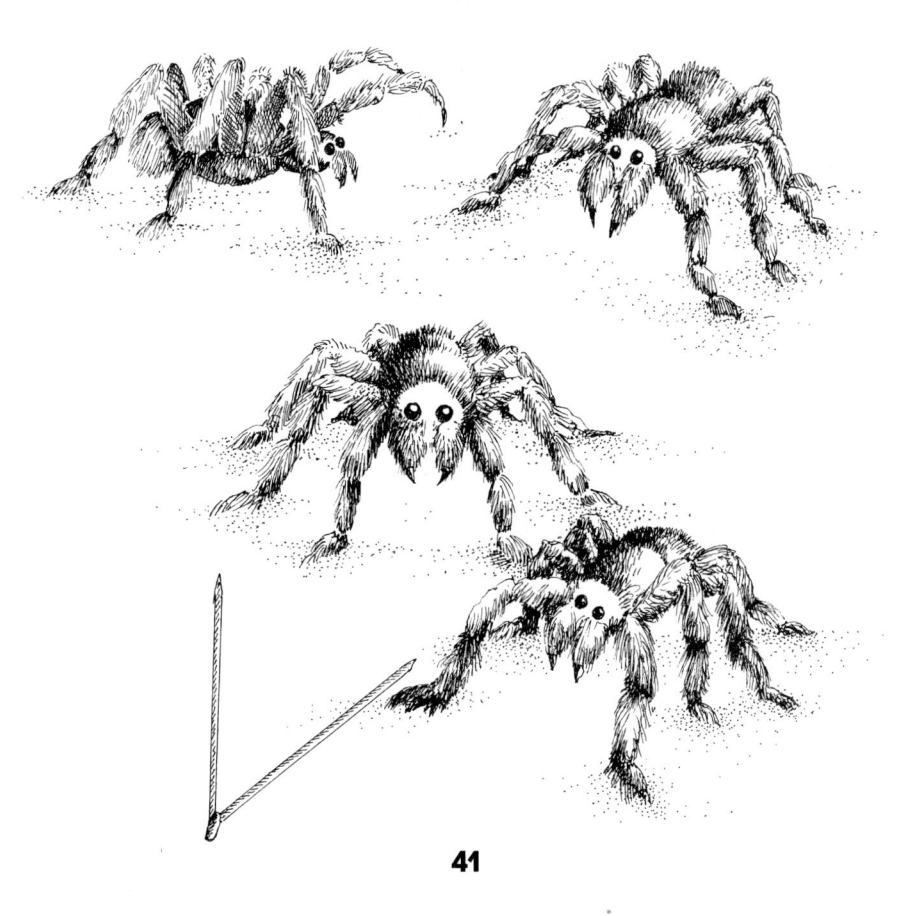

You go out of the room. The next room is huge. It is so big that your Globe of Everlasting Light cannot show you all the walls. All around it is dark and gloomy. You listen. What is that sound? Something is scratching on the floor, or is it the sound of many little feet on the stone?

Then you see black shapes move out of the darkness into your light. Spiders the size of a dinner plate rush at you. Multiplying Hound leaps at them. There are too many. They are the Divider Spiders! Your only hope is to scare them off by some neat dividing. Do you have the Pair of Dividers? If you do, you can go to **42**. If not you will need to go to **36** to get them.

You will have to do these divisions to beat off the Divider Spiders. You take out the Dividers. You hold them up. You hear the voice of the Divider:

Division by a single digit
411 divided by 3 is written

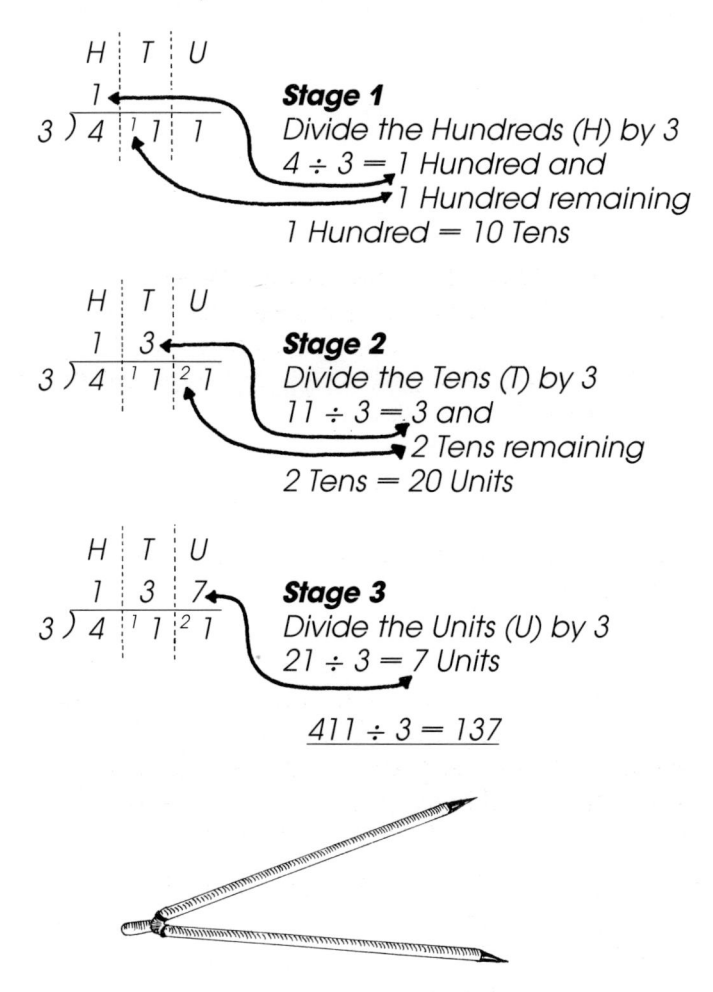

```
    H   T   U
    1
 3 ) 4   1   1
```
Stage 1
Divide the Hundreds (H) by 3
4 ÷ 3 = 1 Hundred and
1 Hundred remaining
1 Hundred = 10 Tens

```
    H   T   U
    1   3
 3 ) 4  ¹1  ²1
```
Stage 2
Divide the Tens (T) by 3
11 ÷ 3 = 3 and
2 Tens remaining
2 Tens = 20 Units

```
    H   T   U
    1   3   7
 3 ) 4  ¹1  ²1
```
Stage 3
Divide the Units (U) by 3
21 ÷ 3 = 7 Units

$$411 \div 3 = 137$$

Now do these sums. Some of them have been written in words as well as numbers. Write down what the sum is before you try to do it. They are all single digit division!

1 2$\overline{)468}$ =

2 3$\overline{)258}$ =

3 There are 735 spiders. You decide that you will split them into 3 groups. Write down the sum you will do and then the answer.

   Sum: Answer:

4 7$\overline{)833}$ =

5 Six of the spiders are left. The others have been driven off. Multiplying Hound decides to multiply them! What will he have to multiply them by to make 354 spiders? Write down the sum you will have to do and then the answer.

   Sum: Answer:

If your answers were correct go to **81**. If you made a mistake go to **139**.

43

   One of the little men comes forward. He only comes up to your chest. He looks very pale and thin. Yet there is a power about him. He speaks: 'I am the seventh son of a seventh son. I have the power of the 77th. You must be the Chosen One promised us!'.

   He then goes on to tell you that RA, an evil being, has taken over the Pyramid. Once (in the days of yore!), only the High Graph Priests lived in the Pyramid. They went their own way trying out new maths ideas. Now RA is forcing them to burn numbers and maths books. RA has taken their children and locked them up in the Mummy's tomb. (This is RA's idea of a joke - a Mummy for the children.) The Mummy will kill the children unless the Priests do as RA says. Go to **44**.

44

The High Graph Priest asks you to help.

You can agree to help - **83** - or say that there is no way you are going to get killed by a Mummy - **95**.

45

You look into a small gap in the rock face. There is a small cave here. It has a sandy floor. The sand looks very deep. The cave has a high, wide roof. The walls narrow down so that the floor has a smaller area. The room is shaped like an inverted cone. Pick out which of these shapes is like that. Write the name of each shape below.

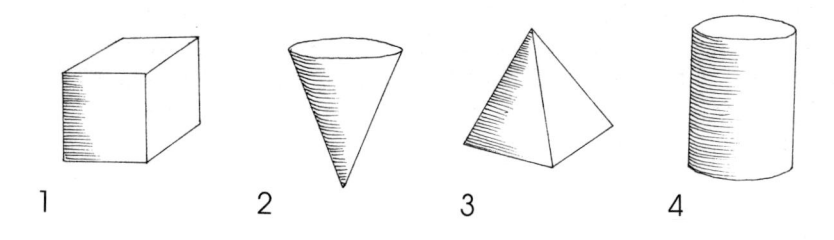

1   2   3   4

1 _____ 2 _____ 3 _____ 4 _____

Now go to **56**.

46

Adder is still with you. He is small and so he can stay curled up out of harm's way. He can help here. You add 4 + 7. The frame of the Globe tilts. If you can add all the numbers, the Globe will fall out. It may help you to write the sums like this   4   on a piece of paper.
                                                    + 7

The first sum has been done for you.

4 + 7 = 11	12 + 6 =	56 + 73 =	123 + 45 =
3 + 6 =	17 + 2 =	21 + 54 =	78 + 27 =
4 + 2 =	38 + 7 =	52 + 36 =	45 + 326 =

Check your answers. If you were correct, go to **68**.
If you made any mistakes, go to **6**.

47

You step into the cave. At once the Sand starts to shift. You sink up to your knees. Then the Sand seems to run out of the bottom of the cave. You are taken along with the Sand. You try to grab at the cave wall. Too late! You are falling, along with a rush of Sand, into a hole in the cave floor! Go to **48**.

48

The Sand takes you along with it. You rush into the hole as though you were going down a water slide. You travel along a narrow tube of stone. Then it opens out again. You are dumped into a pile of Sand. This room is like a cone the right way up! You have gone from the top of a giant Sand Timer to the bottom. The Sand went from one cone to the other. It is the Sand of Time. Time is running out for you. You will have to stop RA soon.

Then you feel something odd. You seem to be forgetting your numbers. The Sand of Time can make you forget. RA is trying one last time to beat you. You begin to forget what you are here for. You will have to do something before you forget and get lost in Time. Go to **54**.

49

You decide to use the Sword on the Hound. You take out the Sword as the Hound bounds toward you. You swipe at its left head. All at once two heads appear where there had been one! The Hound now has three heads! The Sword really does multiply things. This is not what you need here. Just as you are about to run back the Sword starts to glow. You see new words on the Sword. They say:

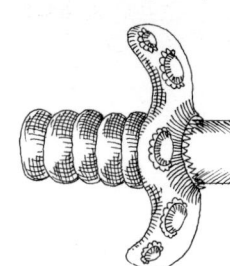

Multiplying by a single digit

You swish the Sword again. You see some more words and numbers.

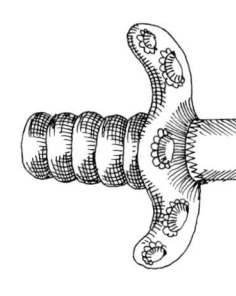

To multiply 235 by 4

```
H  T  U
2  3  5
   ×  4
      0
   2
```
a) Multiply Units 4 × 5 = 20
   (2 Tens 0 Units)

```
H  T  U
2  3  5
   ×  4
   4  0
1  2
```
b) Multiply 4 × 3 = 12 Tens
   12 Tens + 2 Tens = 14 Tens
   (1 Hundred 4 Tens)

```
H  T  U
2  3  5
   ×  4
9  4  0
1  2
```
c) Multiply 4 × 2 = 8 Hundreds
   8 Hundreds + 1 Hundred
   = 9 Hundreds
   (9 Hundreds 4 Tens 0 Units)

You can use this to attack the Hound - go to **91** - or carry on fighting with the Sword - **32**.

The Spell of Areas

To find the area of a square or rectangle.

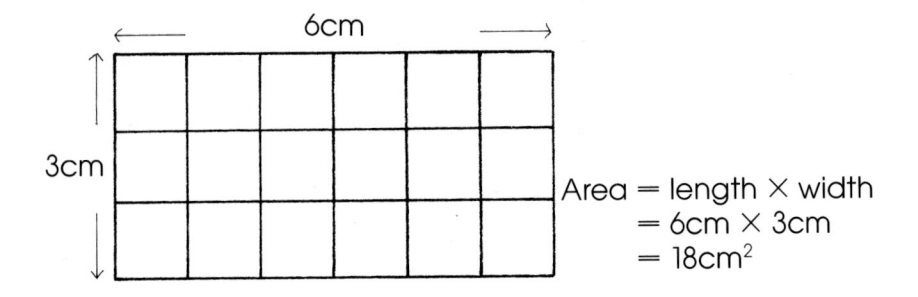

Area = length × width
= 6cm × 3cm
= 18cm^2

This is a compound shape.

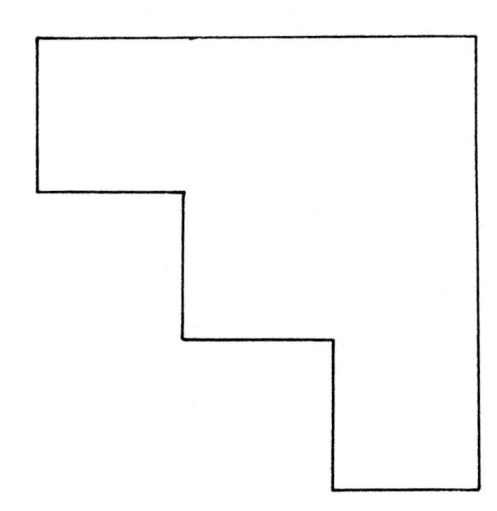

To find the area of a compound shape we divide the shape up into rectangles.

6cm

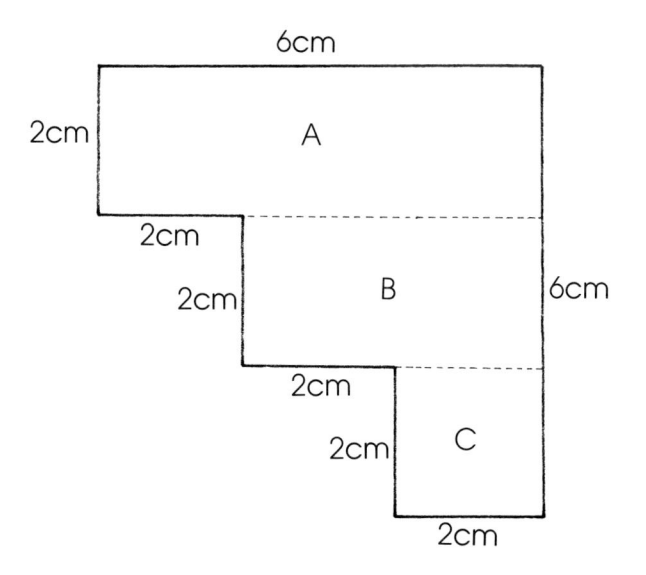

2cm A

2cm

2cm B 6cm

2cm

2cm C

2cm

Area of A = 6cm × 2cm = 12cm²
Area of B = 4cm × 2cm = 8cm²
Area of C = 2cm × 2cm = 4cm²
Total area = A + B + C = 24cm²

51

The rooms look like this. Find the areas of the shapes. *They are not drawn to scale.* You can use the Spell of Areas at **50** to help you.

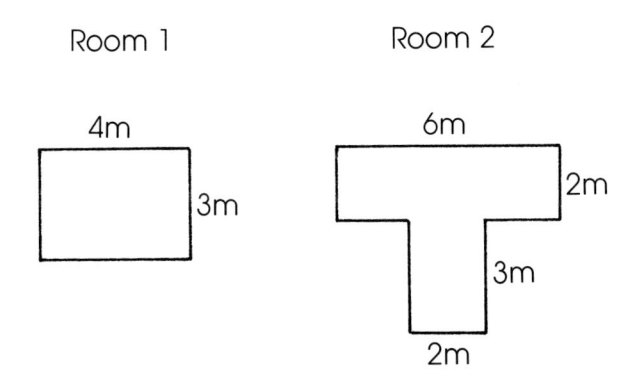

Room 1

4m
3m

Room 2

6m
2m
3m
2m

Room 3
3m
1m
3m
2m

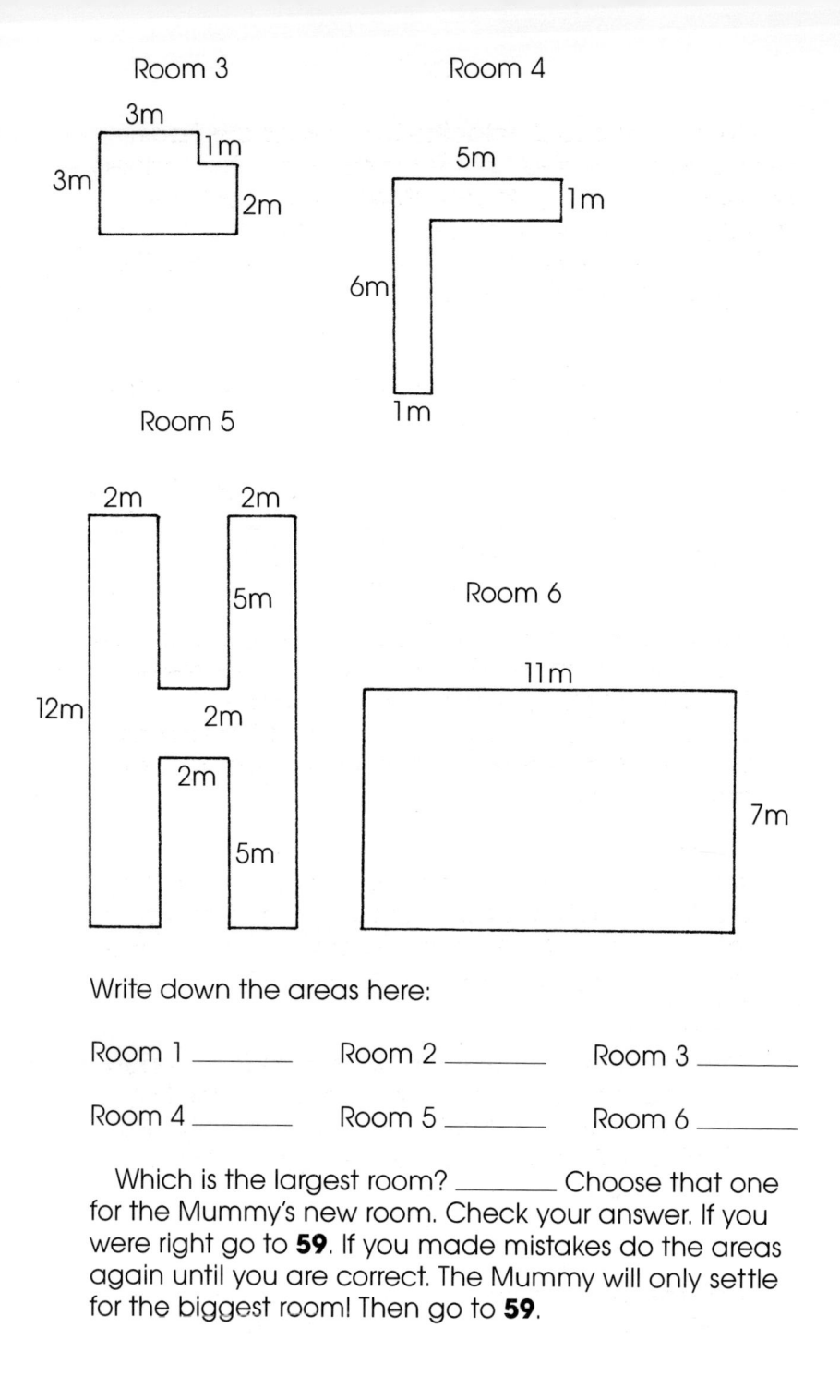

Room 4
5m
1m
6m
1m

Room 5
2m   2m
5m
12m   2m
2m
5m

Room 6
11m
7m

Write down the areas here:

Room 1 _____   Room 2 _____   Room 3 _____

Room 4 _____   Room 5 _____   Room 6 _____

Which is the largest room? _____ Choose that one for the Mummy's new room. Check your answer. If you were right go to **59**. If you made mistakes do the areas again until you are correct. The Mummy will only settle for the biggest room! Then go to **59**.

A few things could help. The best things are Adder because he can add up the numbers and the Dividers because they can help you divide. To work out the average of 2, 3 and 10, you add up the numbers (2 + 3 + 10 = 15). There are three numbers so you divide the answer by three (15 ÷ 3 = 5).

1   Find the average (mean) of these numbers:

    4, 2, 10, 8 _____

2   Some of the bags of coins have fallen open. You see that they have coins worth 10p, 25p, 40p, 20p, 30p in them. Find the average value of the bags.

    _____

3   The Witch sends out five red pulses of light. She uses the light to melt some of the coins. It takes these times to melt a sack of coins: 25 seconds, 27 seconds, 29 seconds, 32 seconds and 22 seconds. What is the average time for the pulses of light to melt the coins?

    _____

4   You see that the Witch has three broomsticks. They are 135cm, 129cm and 141cm long. What do you think would be the length of a broom that was the average length of these three brooms?

    _____

5   You notice that some more bags have fallen open. This time you count the number of coins. You find that the bags have the following number of coins: 48, 50, 51, 47, 54, 50. Find the average number of coins in the sacks.

    _____

Now check your answers. If you were right in them all, go to **71**. If you made any mistakes, go to **8**.

53

You say 'seven'. The little men look as if that might be part of the answer. It is still not quite right. Go back to **20** and choose one of the other numbers there.

54

You can:

- try to get out of the Sand - **61**
- try to find something to help in the Sand - **72**
- do a Sand of Time problem - **58**

55

You go over to the corner of the cave. The smell gets even worse. There are bat droppings all over the floor of the cave. You see the shine of a long metal rod in the muck. You ask Number Cruncher to get it for you. He is most upset. Multiplying Hound pretends that he does not hear. In the end you have to dig it out yourself.

You find some old bones on the ground. It is another adventurer. How did he die you wonder? In the bones of his hand you find the metal rod. You clean it up.

You use a bit of old rag that you were carrying the Skeletons' items in. The metal rod turns out to be a sword. It has this written on it:

Whosoe'er findeth this Sword shall be the Master of Time

Write down Time Sword on your Equipment List, strap the Sword to your back and go to **66**.

56

You should have written:

1 cube
2 cone
3 pyramid
4 cylinder

Check out your answers and then go to **47**.

57

The way ends in a pile of rock. This was not the way marked 1927! You cannot get past. Go back to **100** and choose again.

58

You will have to solve the Sand of Time problem. Do you have the Message from the High Graph Priest? Check your Equipment List. If you do not have it, look in the Sand at **72**.

Here is the problem:

The Sand falls at the rate of 125g a second. It has been falling for fourteen (14) seconds. You will need to work out what the problem is asking. Write out the sum you have to do for each question. Then write the answer.

                          Sum   Answer

1   How much Sand has fallen?

2   How many seconds are needed for 5000 grams to fall?

3   If there were 5000 grams of Sand to start with how much is left after 14 seconds?

Check that your sums were right and then that the answers were correct. Get some help if you made mistakes. Then go to **65**.

59

    The Mummy is very pleased with its new room. The Mummy shows you a small door set in the wall. The children have been kept hidden inside a small cave. They are very pleased to see you. The Mummy tells the High Graph Priest that he can take the children. They all go off together. The Priest wishes you luck in your Quest to find RA.

    'RA!? You are going to find RA?', the Mummy roars. 'He is the one who made me keep the children.' You explain that you are going to find him and stop him taking away all the mathematics.

The Mummy scratches its head. 'What is wrong with taking away the mathematics?', it asks. You can tell it at **63** or shrug your shoulders and go on with your Quest - **12**.

60

It will help if you have read The Book of Numbers. Go and find a copy! If you want to go on with Number Quest without reading The Book of Numbers go to **24**.

61

You try to climb out. The Sand keeps slipping down. You cannot get out, you keep falling back. Back to **54** and try again.

62

You go back, back down the passage. You check the sums of the five ways. You try the other four ways. They are all dead ends. You will have to go back and find a way to go on - **143**.

63

You try to tell the Mummy why we need mathematics and numbers. Write down as many ideas or reasons as you can. Think of the everyday reasons we need numbers or mathematics and the kinds of jobs that need numbers or mathematics.

When you have written as many reasons as you can go to **28**.

64

You leave the Mace on the ground. Then you get ready to leave the Throne Room. Go to **82**.

65

Well done! You have solved the problem of the Sand of Time. All the Sand falls out of another hole. This hole is too small for you. As the Sand clears you see a doorway in the side of the cone-shaped cave. You also see a small window set in the other side of the cave. You can go out of the door - **72** - or look into the window - **101**.

66

You see that the cave has an exit at the back. You run to it. You hold your nose. The smell is becoming too much! You come out into a long, high passage. As you walk down the passage you hear the high pitched squeak of bats. It is a pity that the bats in the Pyramid are not friendly. RA has turned them into evil Bracket Bats and they are heading for you! You will have to drive them off.

Check your Equipment List. Do you have the Bracket Boomerangs? If you do, go to **67**. If you do not, go to **140**.

67

You can throw the Bracket Boomerangs at the bats to drive them away. You need to do these sums before you can use them:

Work out the sum in the brackets first!

1 (24 × 3) − 15   =

2 67 − (44 ÷ 11)   =

3 (68 + 24) ÷ 4   =

4 (35 × 10) − 55   =

5 7 × (12 − 5)   =

6 18 of the Bats fly up to the roof. 9 of them then fly off down the passage. How many are left? This group is joined by 7 times their number. Write down the sum, using brackets for the first part:

   Sum   =

7 (90 − 5) × 100   =

8 121 ÷ (21 − 10)   =

9 (5 + 7) × (4 − 2)   =

10 Suddenly, 12 Bats start to go for you. Then 3 of them fly off towards Number Cruncher. 8 other bats go to Multiplying Hound. He drives off 5 of these. Divide the number of bats that are still going for you by the number of bats that are still going for Hound. Write down the sum with brackets and then the answer.

   Sum   =

Now check your answers. If you were correct, go to **79**. If you made mistakes, do the sums again until they are correct (get some help if you need to). Then go to **79**.

68

At last, the Globe falls out. You catch it. Adder is very pleased with himself. The Globe of Everlasting Light will light your way inside the Pyramid. Write down Globe on your Equipment List. Then go on to **74**.

69

You go down the path to the right. You see something shine white on the ground. You look more closely and see that it is a bone. In fact it is a human bone! As you go on down the passage you see more and more human bones. What can be at the end of the passage?

At last you reach the end. There you see a stone door. It is locked. Next to the door is a slot. It might take a coin. Check your Equipment List. If you have a Coin go to **104**. If you do not have any Coins go to **16**.

70

You go out of the cave. You go down a short path and come to a gold door. There is a big door knocker on the door. It looks like a number 8. You knock on the door. It opens. You step inside. You are in RA's Den. Go to **73**.

71

The Witch is angry that you know how to average. 'RA will see to you!', she screams. Then she takes one of the broomsticks and flies off. She leaves the Mace behind. You can pick it up - **107** - or leave it there - **64**.

72

You dig in the Sand. You find a metal tube. Inside the tube is a scrap of paper. You can look at the paper at **118**. When you have been to **118** go to **54**. (Make a note of these numbers!)

73

RA's Den is huge. Across the room you see RA. You have finally met him! He is an evil-looking wizard. 'So! You dare try to stop the great RA! I have come back from the dead to destroy the Numbers of the World. You have met many of my creatures. You have even beaten my Dragon. But you will not beat RA so easily!'

As he speaks RA points at you with his finger. A red beam of light strikes the floor in front of you. A crack of energy opens up the floor. Deeper cracks appear. You will have to cross over the cracks to get to RA. You will need to use numbers to cross the cracks. You can do this with a 'Crossnumber'. This is like a crossword, but using numbers. Go to **84**.

74

You look around the room. You can see one door. You look out and see Counting Camel chewing. The door you can see is the one you came in through. You look at the other walls of the antechamber. One seems to show the outline of a door. You try to get it open. You break a fingernail! Then you notice a number by the side of the door outline. It is the number 21. On the floor, in front of the door outline you see some squares. Each square slab has a number on it. They look like this:

a	28	45	8	2	34
b	56	87	38	124	112
c	3	217	67	7	29
d	14	53	3	19	4

You need to step on some squares to open the door. Choose one number from each row. Start at row a. You need to end up with the number 21. The Number Cruncher's Code will help you. Check your Equipment List. If you have the Code go to **75**. If you do not, make a note of this number and go to **85**. When you have got the Code come back here.

75

Look at the Code at **76**. When you have worked out what to do write down the numbers of the squares you need to step on. Write one from each row.

a =   b =   c =   d =

If you were right go to **97**. Keep trying until you get the right numbers if you were wrong.

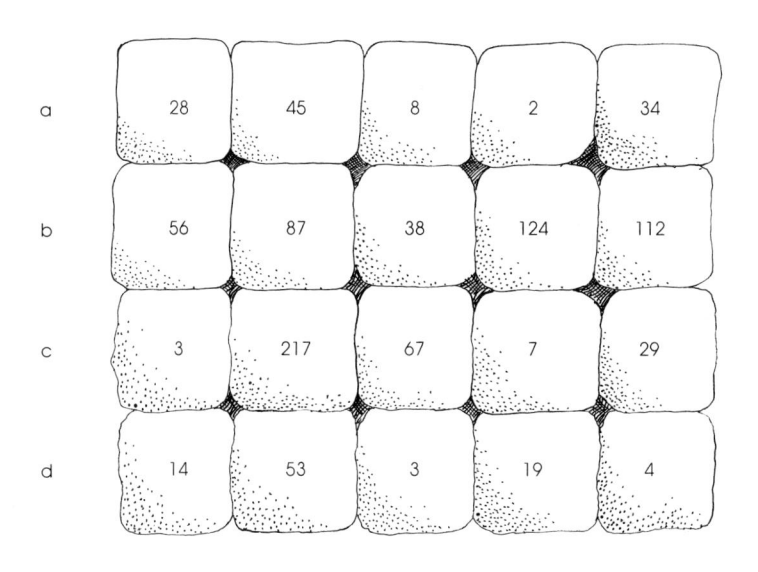

a	28	45	8	2	34
b	56	87	38	124	112
c	3	217	67	7	29
d	14	53	3	19	4

76
Number Cruncher's Code

Here is a way to work out the floor code in the antechamber. You need to find one number (slab) from each row. First take away one of the numbers in row b from one of the numbers in row a (a-b). If you chose the right numbers you will now have one of the numbers in row c (a − b = c). Then take *that* number and multiply it with one of the numbers in row d (c × d). If your numbers are correct you should have 21! The Code is a − b = c then c × d = 21.

77

The answer to 1 was 77. The answer to 11 × 7 is 77. You were told to go to 77. This is strange. Now do these sums:

```
   56          38          98         123
 + 21        + 39        − 21        −  46        10 )‾7‾7‾0‾
 ____        ____        ____        ____
```

What do all the answers come to? _____

You see that the distance between RA's Altar and RA's Den is 77 as well (look at **110** to remind yourself if you need to). The steps must go down to RA's Altar. You start to go down the stairs. Go to **78**.

78

The stairs wind round and round. You count them. There are 77 steps! As you get near the bottom of the stairs you hear something. It is the sound of drums. There is also some chanting. As you get closer you can hear the words more clearly.

Seven times seven we turn around,
Seven times seven we kiss the ground,
Seven years and seven more,
Seven and seven from days of yore!

You are not sure what it all means. (Finding out what 'days of yore' means will help.)

You come to a huge oak door. You cannot open it. On the door you see these numbers. It is the seven times table. You will have to finish the table before the door will open.

1 × 7 = 7   4 × 7 =   7 × 7 =   10 × 7 = 70
2 × 7 = 14   5 × 7 = 35   8 × 7 =   11 × 7 = 77
3 × 7 =   6 × 7 =   9 × 7 =   12 × 7 =

When you have filled in the table you can go to **86**.

79

You fling your Brackets with great skill. Some of the bats are pushed off course. You drive them all away.

The passage is silent once more. You notice that the walls of the cave are black and burnt. You smell a strong burning smell. At the end of the passage you come to three sets of stairs. You can take:

- the one to the left - go to **4**
- the one to the right - go to **33**
- the one in the middle - go to **93**

80

You will have to go back and see if you can find a Coin. Go to **13**.

81

The Divider Spiders are driven back by your dividing. One Divider Spider holds back. It squeaks, 'You will not win the next fight! Prepare to meet your doom!'. Then it scuttles off.

You hear a noise coming from the small room. Could it be the Mummy? Perhaps it is awake. It might come at you like they do in horror films! The noise grows louder. It is a crunching noise. Multiplying Hound goes to one side of the door. You go to the other side. You wait for whatever-it-is to come in. As it does you leap at it with your Sword of Multiplication. (Is this wise after what happened last time?!) Then you stop. A pair of eyes gaze up at you. It is Number Cruncher! He has changed his mind about coming with you. He has followed you all this way.

This is good news. He can help you with the Dragon. You tell him off for creeping up on you, but you are really pleased to see him. You pat him on the head and say 'Good to see you, Cruncher!' (and other such greetings). Write Number Cruncher down on your Equipment List and go to **114**.

82

You take as much of the treasure as you can. You put a few bags of gold Coins into your pockets. You also take some jewels. Next you need to go down the other passage. If you have been there before go back again. Now you have a Coin! Go to **69**.

83

You agree to help. The High Graph Priest is very grateful. He gives you a gift. It is a set of Compass Points. Write down Compass Points on your Equipment List. He also gives Number Cruncher some numbers to crunch. This pleases Number Cruncher but after a while he gets fed up. The numbers are 7, 77, 777 or 7777!

The High Graph Priest will come with you on your way to free the children. Go to **96**.

84

RA's Crossnumber

Work out the sums and
write the numbers in the spaces.

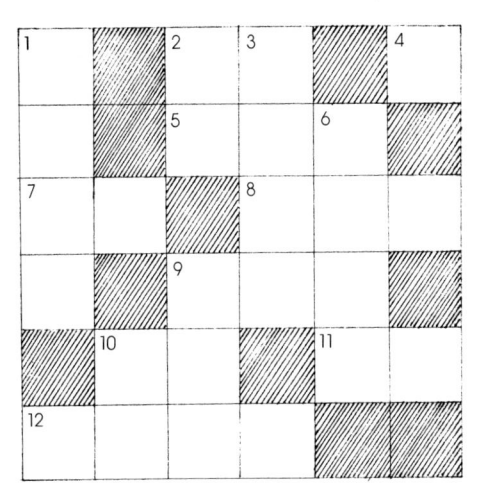

Clues

Down

1. 5 + 60 + 300 + 2000
2. 5 × 9
3. 2.35 am on a 24 hour clock
4. 81 ÷ 9
6. 9732 − 4186
9. The number of days in a year
10. December is the _____ th month of the year

Across

2. (2 × 80) ÷ 4
5. 25 × 21
7. $\frac{1}{2}$ of 124
8. How many pence in £3.50?
9. Add 10 to 344
10. Area of square with 4m sides
11. The number of minutes in an hour
12. The perimeter of a rectangle 400m × 225m

Check to see if you have got your numbers correct. Try again if not. When they are all correct, go to **105**.

85

Number Cruncher has come into the Pyramid with you. He does not like small spaces. After a while he gets scared. He wants to go outside. You tell him to wait outside the Pyramid for you. Before he goes he tells you a Code to help you in the Pyramid. Write Number Cruncher's Code on your Equipment List. You can look at this at **76** at any time. Number Cruncher cannot help you any more here. Go to **25**.

86

The door opens on its own. Inside you see a room lit by torches. The torches are red and give off a thick smoke. At one end of the room is an altar. It is a block of black stone. On the altar you see piles of mathematics books. Around and around the altar go seven little people. They are small with huge eyes.

They turn to look at you. They all chant at the same time, 'Who comes to the seven High Graph Priest's of RA?!'.

Who is RA you think to yourself? What are High Graph Priests?! Whatever they are you must stop them. They are about to burn the mathematics books. You step forward. 'STOP!', you say.

They look at each other. 'Can this be the Chosen One?', the smallest one says. 'We will test him. What is the magic number of our calling?'.

Write down the number here _____. Now go to **20**.

87

You step out on to a wide rocky floor. You are at the top of the Pyramid. You have come out into the open. The smell is the rocks. They have been burnt by Dragon Flame. You are in the Dragon's Lair! This is where the Dragon lives. He flies in and lands on the top of the Pyramid. This flat bit cannot be seen from the base of the Pyramid.

You see ashes and chewed numbers all around. Then you hear a loud flapping of wings. You look up. The Dragon is gliding down to its Lair. Its wings glint in the sun and it colours glow like the sunset. Its face, on the other hand, is evil and twisted. 'So!', it roars. 'You dare to invade my Lair. I told you that I would deal with you!' Go to **89**.

88

You go over and take a look. They seem to have found something. It is a stone tablet with some writing on it. You take a look. It is a spell. It tells you about areas. Write down the Spell of Areas on your Equipment List. You can look at this anytime at **50** (make a note of the number). Now you can go on - **94**.

89

The Dragon spits out a gush of Flame filled with burning Numbers. Number Cruncher begins to crunch them up. Many of them are crunched up but the Flame still gets past him. You need something to protect yourself. Check your Equipment List. Do you have the Number Flame Oil? If you do not, make a note of this number and go to **115**. If you do have the Oil, go to **90**.

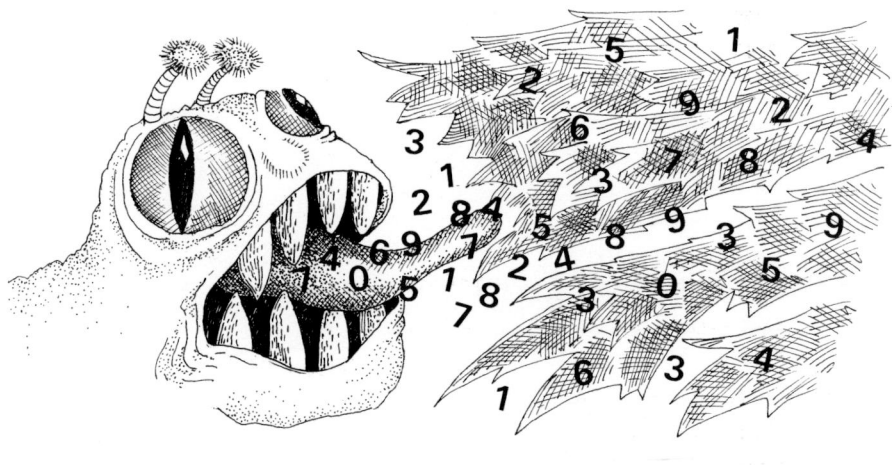

90

You rub some of the Oil on your skin. This stops the worst of the burning. You will have to help Number Cruncher use up the numbers. You must be quick. Time yourself or get someone else to time you.
You must do these sums in less than 120 seconds!
Multiplying Hound can help with some.

Ready ... GO!

1) $7 + 4 =$ ____   2) $17 - 6 =$ ____   3) $5 \times 6 =$ ____

4) $24 \div 6 =$ ____   5) $12 + 34 =$ ____   6) $45 - 23 =$ ____

7) $7 \times 3 =$ ____   8) $120 \div 10 =$ ____

Check your answers. If they were right and you did them in less than 120 seconds, go on to **92**. If you were wrong, keep trying and when you can do them in less than 120 seconds go on to **92**.

91

You use the words from **49** to do these multiplications:

367	642	583	943	455
×5	×4	×6	×3	×2

723	121	432	324
×7	×9	×8	×6

If you were correct, go to **99**. If you were not correct, go to **18**.

92

You stop the Dragon Flame for a while. The Dragon seems to flicker in the air. One minute it is there, the next it is gone. This is very odd. It is as if it is going somewhere else. The Dragon is going in and out of Time. Do you have the Time Clock? Check your Equipment List. If you do go to **7**. If you do not, make a note of this number and go to **115**.

93

You take the stairs in the middle. You go up a winding marble staircase. It seems to go round and round for a long time. At last you see daylight at the top of the stairs. The smell gets stronger. Go to **87**.

94

You will have to find a way across the Lake. Just as you are trying to think of a way, Adder tells you to come and see something. Behind a rock you come across a grid. It glows green and shimmers in the air. Go to **98**.

95

You tell them you will not help. They are sad but they let you go. Go to **96**.

96

You leave the room of RA's Altar through a door shaped like a seven. It leads you down a long passage. You seem to go a long way. At last you feel a breeze on your face. All at once the passage opens out into a vast space. You hold up the Globe of Everlasting Light. You are in a huge underground cave. You cannot see the walls because it is so large. Air seems to blow across the cave. There must be some small holes in the walls.

You look down. Your light sparkles off a shiny surface. It is water. You are in an Underground Lake. The water is icy cold and seems very deep. The Lake stretches across the open space. It feels rather spooky. You look around. Number Cruncher is trying to crunch up some numbers. Multiplying Hound is trying to multiply them. They are not doing very well. You can go over and see what they are up to - **88** - or carry on - **94**.

97

You step on squares 45, 38, 7 and 3 (45 − 38 = 7 then 7 × 3 = 21). There is a screech and a crunching sound. The outline moves. Then an open door appears in the rock face. You see a tunnel ahead through the open door. On the side of the wall as you go in are these words:

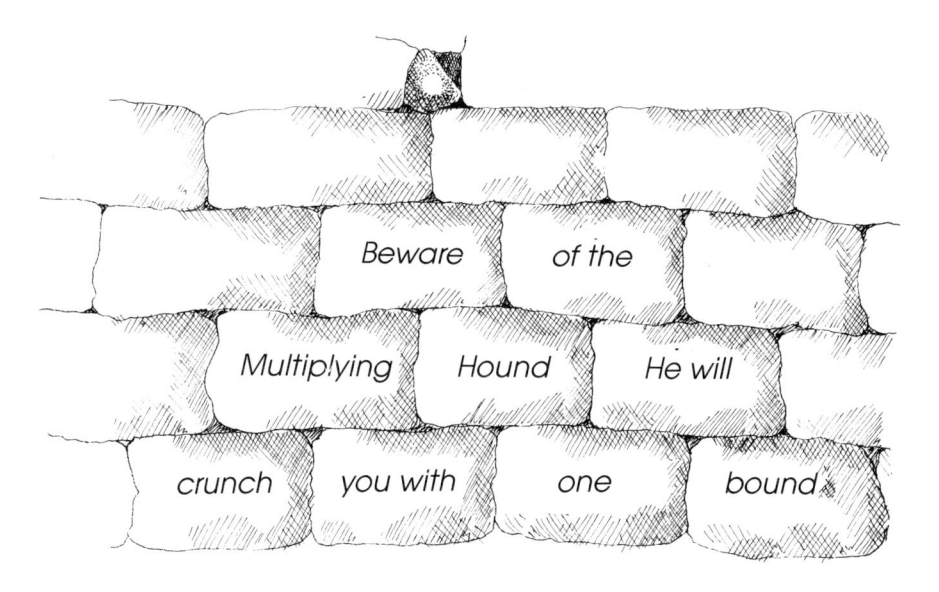

> Beware of the Multiplying Hound He will crunch you with one bound

Above the writing is a small piece of rock sticking out from the rest of the wall. It looks like a button. You can go on - **112** - or press the button - **129**.

The grid looks like this:

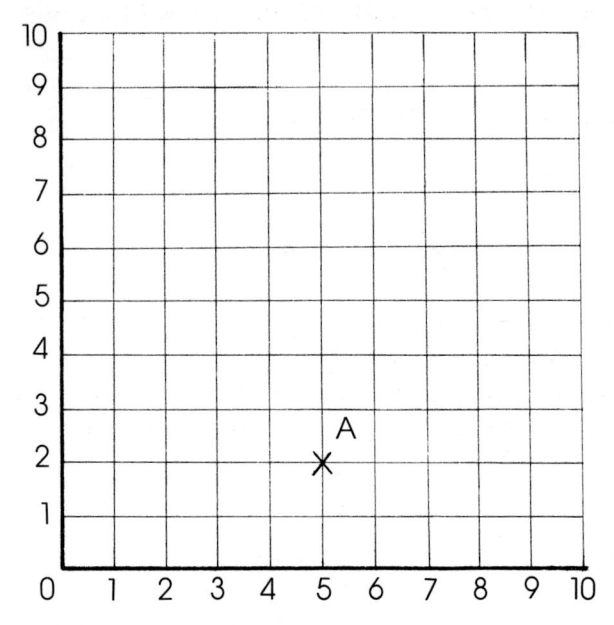

Now read this and mark in some grid co-ordinates.
We use a number pair or co-ordinate to find a point on a grid. Find these co-ordinates on the grid. Mark them with a cross and label them (A, B, C etc). Then join them up by drawing a line between the crosses *in alphabetical order.*

Here are the co-ordinates. The first has been done for you to show you how it works. Always go across first, then up.

A (5, 2)   5 squares across,   2 squares up.

B (1, 2)   F (5, 2)   J (5, 8)

C (3, 0)   G (5, 9)   K (1, 3)

D (7, 0)   H (7, 9)   L (9, 3)

E (9, 2)   I (7, 8)   M (5, 8)

When you have marked the co-ordinates and joined up your crosses, you should see something that will help you.

Write down what it is here _____

Now go to **116**.

99

It took three digit multiplying to stop a three-headed dog. The Hound just wags its tail and lets you past.
In fact it wants to come with you. You have made a friend! Write Multiplying Hound on your Equipment List. Now go to **100**.

100

You go on down the passage. You see some writing on the wall. It says:

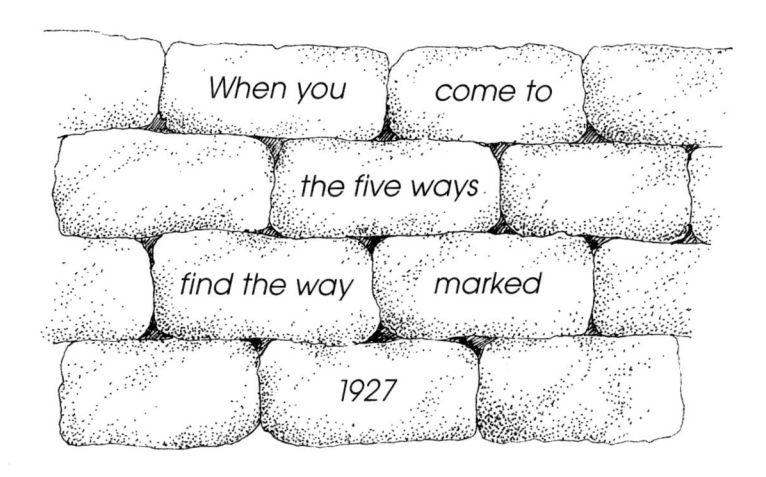

> When you come to
> the five ways
> find the way marked
> 1927

You have not gone far when the passage splits into five ways. Which way will you go? Multiplying Hound jumps up at the front of one of the five ways. Each way has some numbers on its wall. They are sums. You will have to work them out before you can choose the right way. You take out your Sword of Multiplication. This time you see these words:

Multiplying by 2 digits
eg multiply 26 by 35

```
      T  U    Stage 1 Multiplying 26 by 5
      2  6
  ×   3 ⑤
      1  3  0
```

```
      T  U    Stage 2 Multiplying 26 by 30   (3 Tens)
      2  6
  ×  ③  5
      1  3  0   (26 × 5)
      7  8  0   (26 × 30)
```

```
      T  U    Stage 3 Add together your answers
      2  6            from
  ×   3  5
      1  3  0 ← Stage 1 and
  +   7  8  0 ← Stage 2
      9  1  0   (26 × 35)
```

Now you can do the sums of the five ways. The sums are:

Way 1   26   Way 2   43   Way 3   47
       × 35   × 19   × 41
       ____   ____   ____

Way 4   256   Way 5   768
       × 76   × 65
       ____   ____

Now look at your answers. Which way will you take? If you want to take Way 1 or Way 2, go to **17**. If you want to take Way 3, go to **142**. If you want to take Way 4 or Way 5, go to **57**.

101

You look into the gap set in the wall. You see more Sand out of the window. There is nothing else. Go to **70**.

102

You will need the Spell of Areas. Go and find it at **88**. Then come back to **51**.

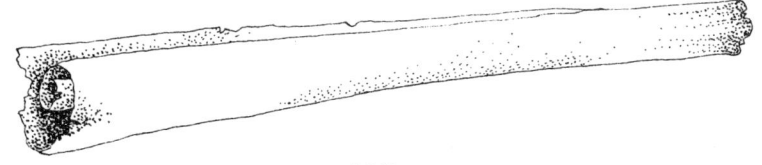

103

Number Cruncher tries to crunch the door down. He hurts his teeth. The door is not made of numbers. Go back to **16** and try again.

104

You take out one of the gold Coins that you found in the Throne Room. You put it into the slot. There is a crunching noise. The stone door moves to one side. A vile smell comes out from behind the black room beyond. Inside in the gloom you can make out some white shapes. You hold up the Globe of Everlasting Light. It is a room full of skeletons. You have found the Skeleton Room.

The Skeletons are pleased to see you. They were buried alive in the Pyramid with RA. They are keen to talk to someone.

Some of them do a kind of dance around you. They shake and rattle their bones. It is the Dance of Numbers. The Skeletons have numbers on their bones. You have to work out what the total number is for each Skeleton while they are dancing. Skeleton 1 has 4 − 2 and 6 on him. This gives a total of 8. Now do these:

Skeleton 2   6 − 4 + 13 − 2 =

Skeleton 3   − 7 + 23 − 15 + 7 =

Skeleton 4   6 − 2 + 23 − 2 =

Check your answers. If you were right the Skeletons stop dancing. They decide it is the interval. They bring around a tray of goods. You can either buy some things - go to **113** - or you can refuse to buy anything - go to **22**.

105

You use the numbers to cross over the cracks in the floor. RA is very angry. 'Now you will die. You will have to solve the Problems of RA! No one has ever done that and lived.'

RA waves his hands. You see some words and numbers appear in the air in front of you. Go to **108**.

106

Counting Camel did not come in with you. He said that there was no way he was going to fight a Dragon. He just refused to move. He said that he might stay and wait for you outside if he felt like it! He cannot help you here! Go to **25**.

107

You pick up the Mace. Write down The Mace of RA on your Equipment List. It might come in handy later. Then you get ready to leave the Throne Room. Go to **82**.

108

Do you have the Message from the High Priest of Number? Check your Equipment List. If you do, go on to **119**. You may like to read the message again at **118**. If you do not have the message, go to **72** and dig in the Sand. Come back here if you have already done the Sand of Time problem.

109

You reach in to take the scroll. It feels dusty and old. You take it out carefully. It is the Distance Chart. Write down Distance Chart on your Equipment List. You can look at this at any time at **110**. Note the number **109** on your Equipment List. Now go back and choose again at **143**.

110

The Distance Chart

The Distance Chart shows distances to places in the Pyramid. The chart shows distances in metres.

	Skeleton Room	Underground Lake	RA's Den	Dragon's Lair	Mummy's Tomb
					220
				163	146
			422	270	490
		416	87	146	74
	302	186	286	168	376
247	144	399	77	153	211

(Rows labelled from top-left diagonal: Throne Room, RA's Altar)

Using the Distance Chart

Let us say the question is how far is it from RA's Den to the Throne Room. You can use your finger like this:

Left hand

Find the Throne Room

Move finger across
302   186   **286**

Right hand

Find RA's Den

Move finger down
422
87
286

Where you meet across and down is the distance - **286**

111

Use the Distance Chart (**110**) to answer these:

1 How far is it from the RA's Altar to RA's Den? _____

2 How far is it from the Underground Lake to the Mummy's Tomb?

_____

3 What is the total distance for each of the following journeys?

   a) RA's Altar ____→ Skeleton Room ____→ Mummy's Tomb

   b) Throne Room ____→ Underground Lake ____→ Dragon's Lair

4   Which is the longest journey, Throne Room to RA's Den or Dragon's Lair to the Underground Lake?
    _____

5   How much further is it? _____

6   Which of the answers is the same as the answer to 11 × 7?
    _____

Now check your answers. If you were correct go to **77**. If you made a mistake go to **121**.

112

You go on down the passage. Just as you reach the end a huge dog stands in front of you. It has two heads!

The heads snarl and bite the air. It is the Multiplying Hound! You will have to multiply some two digit numbers to drive this two-headed beast away. As it gets closer to you do these sums.

34	34	45	50	63
× 2	× 3	× 4	× 5	× 6
___	___	___	___	___

If you were correct, go on to **120**. If you made a mistake, go to **18**.

The Skeletons are happy. Many of them had been shopkeepers before they died. They say that if you buy something they will let you go on to find RA. You will have to work out what you can buy. They show you a tray with these things on it:

Dragon's Blood
36p a pint

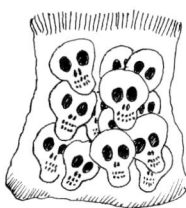

Skelly Jellies
150g packet 35p

Number Flame Oil
£1.28   100g jar

Skeleton Keys
325g box
£1.25

Time Clocks
500g box
75p

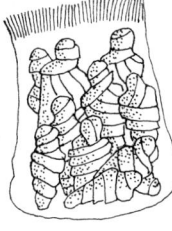

Mummy Mints
72p 250g packet

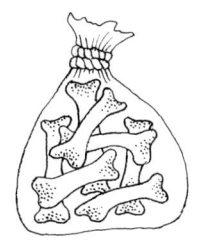

Bone Bags
£2.48
160g bag

1   If you buy one of each of the items what is the total cost?

_____

2   How much change will you get from £1 after buying 2 pints of Dragon's Blood?

_____

3   How much must be added to £5 when you buy 4 jars of Number Flame Oil?

_____

4   How much will it cost to buy 80 Bone Bags? _____

5 The Skeletons say that there is a special offer on Dragon's Blood. If you buy a 4 pint bottle it will cost £1.04. How much do you save if you buy one 4 pint bottle instead of four 1 pint bottles?

   _____

6 How much do the Skeleton Keys and Time Clocks weigh (together)?

   _____

7 What do 2 packets of Skelly Jellies and one packet of Mummy Mints weigh?

   _____

8 Which weighs more, Skeleton Keys and Number Flame Oil or Mummy Mints and Skelly Jellies?

   _____

9 Which four items added together weigh exactly 1kg?

10 After buying one of each of the items the Skeletons give you 6 coins back as change from a £10 note. What are the coins?

   (Use your answer to Q1 as a starting point.)

   _____

Now check your answers. If you were correct, go to **122**. If you made mistakes, go back and redo those questions. Get some help if you need to. Then go on to **122**.

114

   You look around the huge room. No sign of the Divider Spiders. You walk to one side of the room and hold up the light. Nothing. Then you cross to the other side. You see a stone pillar. Next to the pillar is a large hole in the ground. You see some steps going down. Around the pillar are these names. The Underground Lake, RA's Altar, Mummy's Tomb, Dragon's Lair, the Throne Room, the Skeleton Room and RA's Den. To find out which place the stairs lead to, you have to work out the distances between the places.

You can use the Distance Chart at **110** to help you. Now go to **111** to find out where the steps go.

115

You have not chosen to buy the right items from the Skeletons. You will need to go back and get the item you need. First cross off one of the five items from your Equipment List. Then you can go back to **123**. Choose the item you need and write it on your Equipment List. After you have got the item you need, go back to where you were and use it!

116

You should have drawn a boat or something like it. It should look like this.

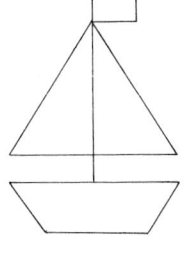

Write Sailing Boat on your Equipment List if you were correct and go on to **117**. If you did not draw a boat go back to **98** and try again. You cannot cross the Lake without a boat.

117

Your picture of the Sailing Boat slowly takes shape. At last it becomes real. You drag it over sand to the side of the Lake. You set off across the Underground Lake.

It is cold on the Lake. A chill wind blows and sends you out into the centre of the Lake. You cannot see the other side of the cave any more. You are sailing in the middle of black water. Which way will you go? Check your Equipment List. Do you have the Compass Points? If you do, go to **124**. If you do not, go to **132**.

118

At first you see nothing, just letters. Then the letters form words.

> You need to solve some problems to beat RA. It will help if you can work out what sum or maths task is asked for. This is not always clear in a problem, but if you can do this it will help you a lot. Sometimes the problem may need a few sums in stages. Write down each sum before you do that part of the problem. Do not be put off by things in the problem that do not tell you about the maths task.

It is a message from the High Priest of Number. Write down Message on your Equipment List and then go back to where you were.

119

This is RA's first problem:

My Dragon was going for a flight to burn the town. He departed from his Lair at 12.08 pm. I rode on his back, as I often do. I came to his Lair 13 minutes early for my ride. The Dragon's Flight took 23 minutes. We got back well pleased with our trip. I stayed and talked to the Dragon for 7 minutes, then took the 4 minute trip back to my Den.

1   What time did I arrive at the Dragon's Lair? _____

2   What time did we get back from our flight? _____

3   What time did I get back to my Den? _____

4   I took the same time to go from my Den to the Dragon's Lair as I did coming back. How long, in total, was I away from my Den?

_____

Check your answers. You will need to get this correct before you can go on. RA will crush you if you do not get it right.

If you were correct, go to **125**.

120

Well done! You have slowed the Hound down, but he still keeps on coming. Do you have the Sword of Multiplication? Check your Equipment List. If you do, go to **49**. If you do not, you may need to go and get it at **129**.

121

You will get lost in the Pyramid if you cannot work out the distances. You will need to go back to **111** and try the questions you got wrong again.

122

Well done! You have worked out many of the prices. The Skeletons say you can have some of the items if you give them Coins. Go to **123**.

123

You can only take five items. Choose five items from Dragon's Blood, Skelly Jellies, Number Flame Oil, Skeleton Keys, Time Clocks, Mummy Mints and Bone Bags. Write the five items you chose on your Equipment List. Then go on to **3**.

124

You take out the Compass Points. They are N (North), NE (North-east), E (East), SE (South-east), S (South), SW (South-west), W (West) and NW (North-west). Write down the points on the Compass. Use letters only. North has been done for you.

Compass

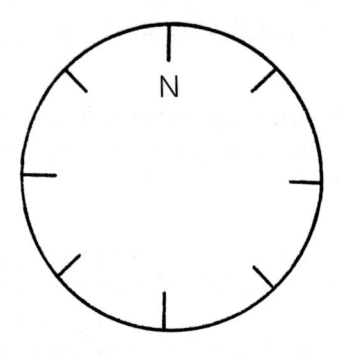

Check your answers. If you put the compass points in the right place you can go to **136**. If you were wrong, go back and correct them. Then go to **136**.

125

'Ha! Some lucky answers!', RA screeches. 'You will fail my second problem!' More words and numbers appear on the wall this time.

This is RA's second problem:

Three of my Skeleton crew went to take some gold from the Throne Room. They took 453 gold coins. They met a Bracket Bat who wanted to take 12 gold coins. First the Skeletons divided the coins between them. Then one of the Skeletons gave 12 coins to the Bat. The Bat dropped 2 coins and then gave half of what he had left to a second Bat.

1 How much money did each of the Skeletons have before they gave any coins to the Bat?

   _____

2 How much money did the Skeleton that gave the money to the Bat have left after he had given the Bat 12 coins?

   _____

3 How much did each Bat get in the end? _____

Check your answers. When you get them correct you can go on to **128**. Get some help if you need to.

Now you have found your bearings you can plot your way down these paths. You need to write down the directions. The first two have been done for you. You had to go North then West to get down the first two paths.

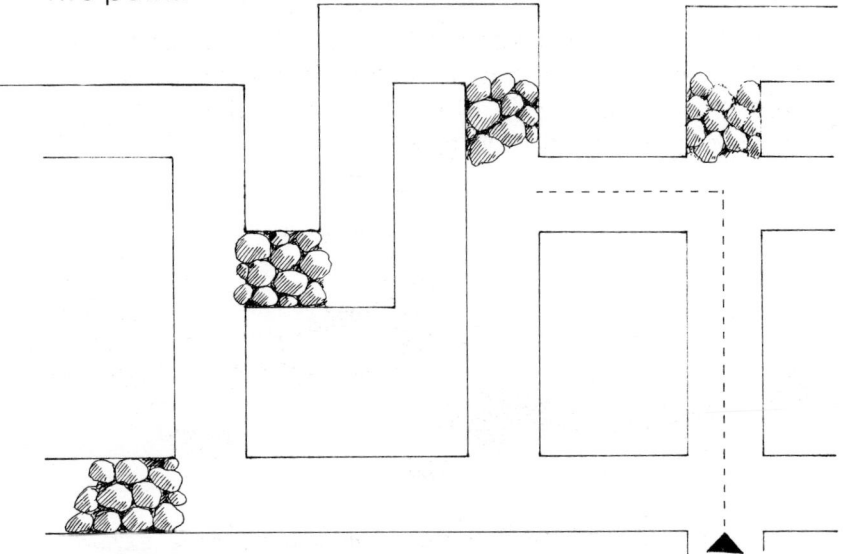

Write down the directions here:

1   North (N)

2   West (W)

3   _____

4   _____

5   _____

6   _____

Check your directions. If you were correct, go on to **127**. If not, keep trying until you find the correct directions.

127

At last you find your way down the passages. Soon you come to a room with the children in it. You see that the Mummy is also there! This must have been the 'thump, swoosh' noise you heard before. It gets up and lumbers over to you. 'What do you want?', it mumbles.

You tell it that you want the Graph children back. The Mummy lets out a roar of rage. Its breath does not smell good. If you have the High Graph Priest with you go to **21**. If you do not go to **2**.

128

RA starts to froth at the mouth in rage! This time the words and numbers appear on the floor.

This is RA's third problem:

I stole some numbers. I made the Priests put the numbers in boxes. They put 36 numbers in each box. There were 32 boxes. Then they put the boxes in 8 rows.

1 How many numbers were there in the 32 boxes?

   _____

2 How many boxes were there in each row?

   _____

3 How many numbers were there in 3 rows?

   _____

Check your answers. When you are correct (get help if you want) go on to **130**.

129

You press the button. A small space appears in the wall. Inside you see a sword. Written on the sword are the words:

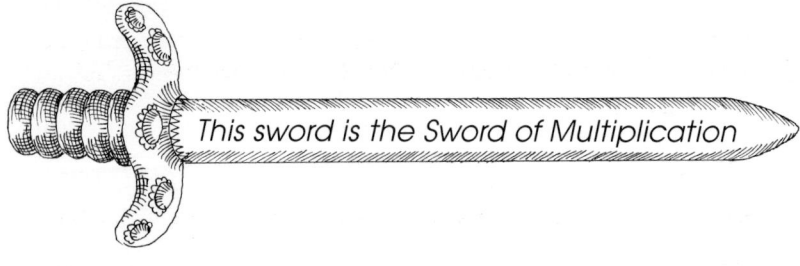

This sword is the Sword of Multiplication

Write Sword of Multiplication on your Equipment List and go to **112**.

130

RA is almost out of control now. He is rolling around on the floor screaming. You think he must be mad. 'Luck! Luck! It must all be luck,' he rages. 'No one will take the numbers back from me!' Then a look of cunning comes over his face. 'This will trick you, human!', he says slyly. Go to **131**.

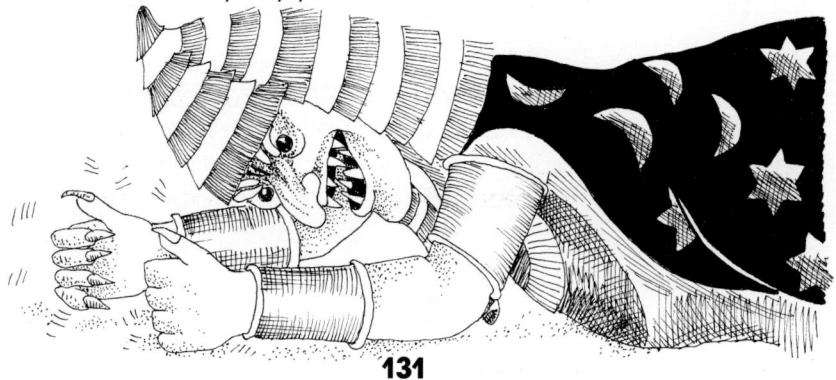

131

This is RA's fourth problem:

My 6 bags of numbers weigh 75g, 75g, 80g, 88g, 92g and 100g.

1. How much do the bags weigh altogether? _____

2. What is the average (mean) weight for the bags?
   _____

3. What is the difference between the heaviest and the lightest bag?
   _____

Check your answers again. If they were correct, go on to **133**.

132

You do not know which way to go. You let the wind blow you where it will. At last you find that you are blown back to the place where you started. You will need some help. You land and go back to RA's Altar. This time you decide you will help the High Graph Priest. Go to **44**.

133

RA looks very weak now. He says nothing. He looks beaten. He seems to fade away. Then he gets more solid again. He makes a final effort. On a table, in the colour of blood, you see RA's last problem. Go to **135**.

134

What?! You were given so many clues! The High Graph Priests throw you onto the altar and burn you along with the books. A painful death! Go back to **77** then try **86** again.

135

This is RA's fifth and final problem:

My Den is 18m long by 10m wide. It has a carpet, made from numbers, 3m long and 2m wide. At one end is my Chair of Mathematics. The Chair is 6m away from the carpet but next to the Table of Operations. The Table is 2m long by 2m wide.

1 What is the area of my Den? _____

2 What is the area of the carpet? _____

3 How many carpets will I need to cover the whole of the floor of the Den?
   _____

4 How many times will I have to walk from the Chair to the carpet to walk the same distance as the length of the room?
   _____

5 How far would I walk if I walked all around the edge of the Den (perimeter)?
   _____

6 Which takes up more area or floor space, the table or the carpet?
   _____

Once more check your answers. If you are correct, go on to **144**.

136

Now you can find your way. You sail North-east. This will take you across the Lake to the Mummy's Tomb. After a while you come to a steep stone wall at one end of the Lake. Set into the wall are some steps. You get out of the boat and climb up the steps, taking care not to fall. You count the steps – guess how many? Yes, that's right, 77!

At the top of the steps you see a vast door. On each side of the door stand two stone figures. Each carries a spear and stands 7ft 7in high. They seem to look down on you. Just as you walk towards the door the figures suddenly bring their spears crashing down across your path. You have stepped on a hidden stone. You cannot get past the spears unless you step on the hidden stone again.

You look down. You see that the stone slabs are numbered from 1 to 100. Which one will you step on? Go to **137**.

137

You step on Number 77. The spears move away. The door slowly opens. You enter the Tomb. It is cold and dank. There is a smell of dead things. You think that a Mummy will leap out at you at any time.
You hear an awful groaning sound from one of the passages. Something thumps down a passage to your right. It sounds as if it is dragging a leg behind it. Thump, swoosh, thump, swoosh. Go to **138**.

You will have to find the children quickly. You see a maze of turnings and twistings. You will have to use your Compass Points (check your Equipment List). You need to take your 'bearings'. This will help you decide which direction to take. Look at these 'bearings' from your Compass Points kit:

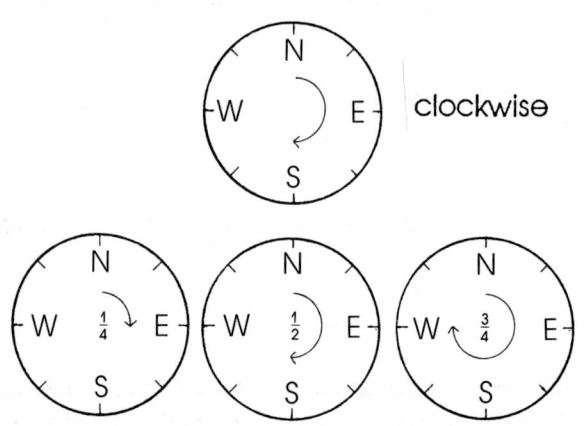

clockwise

If you stand facing North and turn clockwise for ¼ of a turn you are facing East. This is shown in one of the drawings above. A turn is sometimes called 'going through a revolution', because you 'revolve' around. Clockwise is in the direction the hands of a clock go round. Anti-clockwise is the opposite direction.

Now find your bearings in the Tomb by answering these questions. The compass drawings above will help you.

1 If you stand facing North and turn clockwise through ¾ of a revolution, in which direction are you facing?

   _____

2 If you stand facing West and turn clockwise through ½ of a revolution, in which direction are you facing?

   _____

3 If you stand facing South and turn anti-clockwise through $\frac{3}{4}$ of a revolution, in which direction are you facing?

_____

4 If you face West and turn clockwise to face South, through how much of a revolution have you turned?

_____

5 If you face South and turn clockwise through $\frac{1}{4}$ revolution, in which direction are you facing?

_____

If you were correct in your answers you can go to **126**. If you made a mistake go to **14**.

139

The Divider Spiders crawl all over you. They start to think about biting. Go back and correct your answers (**42**) before you are bitten to death.

140

You will have to go back and get the Bracket Boomerangs. The Mummy would have given them to you. Go back to **63**. Tell the Mummy about mathematics then go to **29**. When you have the Bracket Boomerangs you can go to **67**. (Make a note of all these numbers! **63**, then **29** and then **67**.)

141

'Well', says the Dragon, 'That's all very well. But it is only part of my riddle!'. You think that this is most unfair. The Dragon did not say that there were to be *two* riddles! You do not have any time to make a protest. The second riddle is upon you. Go to **23**.

142

Well done! This is the way marked 1927. Multiplying Hound wags his tail (and his heads!).

You go down this passage. It gets wider as you go further down. At last you come to a dead end. Set into the wall facing you is a large bowl. It has water in it and a spout. Above the spout is the head of a Dragon.

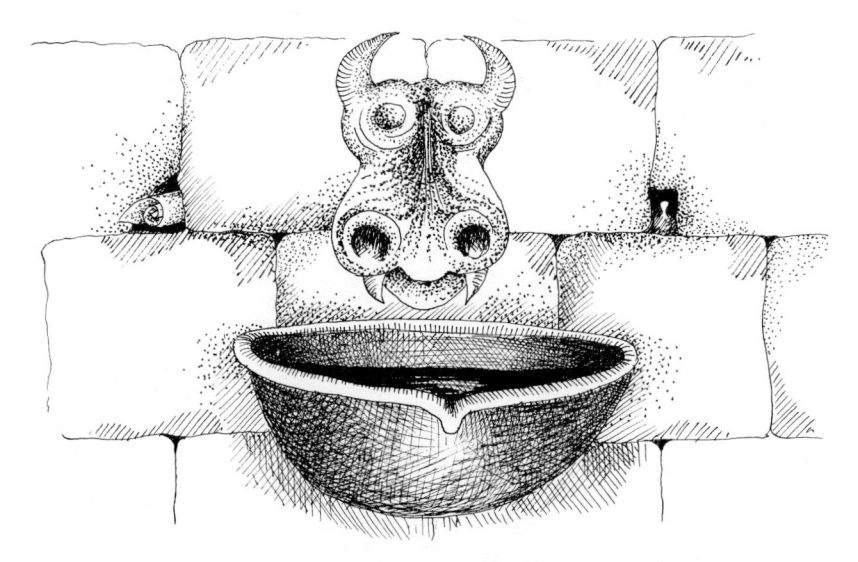

It is carved out of stone with two red eyes set into the stone. On one side of the water bowl is a small hollow set in the wall. You see a scroll in the hollow. On the other side of the Dragon's head you see a small switch set into the wall. Go to **143**.

143

What are you going to do? You can:

- take the scroll - **109**
- press the switch - **11**
- go back down the passage - **62**

144

RA fades away. You hear a cry of anger. Then RA is no more. You have won. The Numbers of the World are safe. You have proved yourself to be a Master of Mathematics. You can be proud of your number work.

Number Cruncher is very pleased. Lots more numbers for him to crunch. Multiplying Hound can multiply the numbers for Number Cruncher. You quickly find a way out of the Pyramid. The townspeople (and Counting Camel) are there to greet you. Your adventure is over. You are a hero.

The end, but perhaps one day ...?

EQUIPMENT LIST

Adventurer, here is your Equipment List. Use it when you write down equipment you find on your journey.

If you stop reading write down the number you are on. Then you will know where to start next time.

Equipment   **Story number**